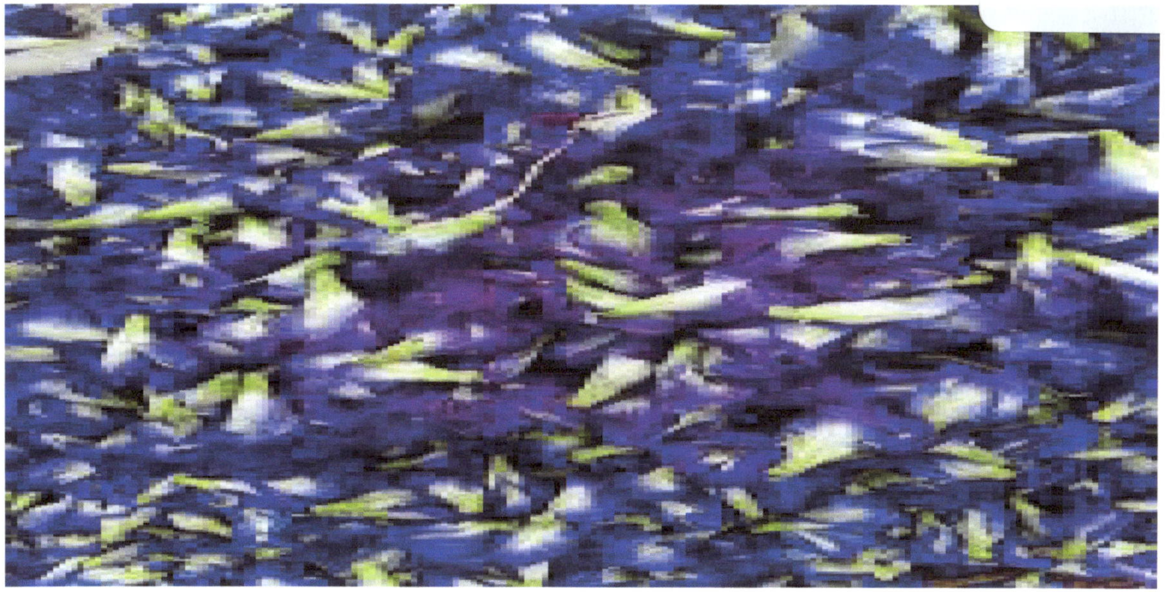

BEAUTY OF NATURE

FLOWER

INTRODUCTION

Nature has been the source of our delight. It is the reason for our life and sustenance. The earth is beautiful because of nature. It is a creation of the God himself. Hence, it is all beauty. In the Holy Bible, we see the beautiful Garden of Eden as an example of natural bliss. Nature is a gift of God towards all living creatures on the earth. There is no one who is not daily helped by the goods of nature. Nature is significant to the development of life. Everything you feel and see around, including Mountains, Forests, Rivers, Birds, Plants, Animals, Air, etc. – all are a part of the beauty of nature.

What is the importance of flowers in nature? Besides adding color, texture and biodiversity to gardens and ecosystems, flowers are botanically important structures and essential sources of food for many organisms. The flower is an important means of attracting pollinator to a plant, which is necessary in order for the plant to produce seeds, reproductive structures that allow a species to exist generation after generation.

The importance of flowers in nature cannot be overstated. Without flowers, there would be no fruit, grains, nuts or berries, as these are the ripened products of a successfully fertilized flower. These foods that are critical sources of calories and nutrients for a wide variety of organisms help support the biodiversity of our planet. Flowers have the power to lift moods, decrease depression and improve creative performance. Clearly, flowers are important in nature – and to humans – in many different ways. Most of the food that humans, insects and animals eat comes from angiosperms, or plants that make flowers.

Vegetables like peas, tomatoes, peppers, sweet corn and broccoli are produced by angiosperms. Grains such as wheat, rice, barley, oats and rye are products of angiosperms, and fruits like apples, oranges and bananas all come from flowering plants too. Even plants grown to feed livestock often make flowers. Forage crops such as soybeans, clovers, alfalfas and vetches are all flowering plants. Most of the flowering plants that are grown for food, forage and fiber are bought and sold internationally, and our global economic markets are based on the trading of goods that are related directly to the production of flowering plants.

Humans can enjoy almost every aspect of flowering plants. Their fragrances and colors are stimulating to the senses, they produce abundant food from most every part, and many flowering plants even have medicinal properties. Flowering trees produce wood for crafting and building. Many animals that depend on flowering plants are edible for humans as well. Even ancient angiosperms that lived long before humans are a boon to us, since they became fossil fuels that power human technology. Flowers play a crucial role in our lives; they have been used for generations to express the thoughts and feelings words cannot fully explain. We are also connected to plants and flowers, and some of the benefits have been passed to the next generation and will always be. What is the importance of flowers in our lives, you wonder? They help release anxiety and tension, and global researchers agree that stress relief benefits from plants and flowers. When we are in a bright environment with a soothing atmosphere, our brains release happy (feel-good) hormones. The effect of feel-good hormones makes us feel good about ourselves and enlighten our hearts with love, laughter, and happiness.

The use of flowers for medicinal purposes has also been practiced since ancient times. This is the reason why most of the medicines are made from specific plants or flowers. Some of the most popular medicinal flowers are lavender, begonia, carnations, gardenia, and jasmine, among others. Flowers signify strength, purity, consciousness. Decorating your interior and exterior spaces with flowers importance and plants also go a step further and bring up positive vibrations and attract prosperity, health, happiness, and love. All because you shared the same space with a beautiful and fragrant flower! Anyone can surprise their loved ones with a bunch of flowers to express their thoughts and wishes.

 What is the importance of flower in our life? Flowers not only add color, texture, and biodiversity to gardens and environments, they are also an important structure for plant and an essential food source for many organisms. Flowers are attracting pollen substances to plants, and plants need to produce seeds. The reproductive structure, allow seeds to exist for generations. Flowers can also protect growing seeds and successfully pass genetic material to the next generation. It is impossible to overstate the importance of flowers in nature. Without flowers there are no grains, nuts, or berries, because these are the mature products of successfully fertilized flowers. These foods, which are essential source of calories and nutrients for a wide variety of organisms, help support our planet's ecosystem. Here we discuss some Flowers which enrich our beauty of nature.

<u>LOTUS</u>

From new life to death, from purity to passion, flowers have had many meanings in myths and legends. Swelling from tender bud to full bloom, flowers are associated with youth, beauty, and pleasure. As they wilt and die, flowers represent fragility and the swift passage from life into death.   The lotus flower is an aquatic perennial. Sometimes mistaken for the water-lily, the lotus has a distinctively different structure. It also only comes in pink hues or white, whereas the lily comes in many different colors. The roots are implanted in the soil of a river or pond, and the leaves float on the surface.

The lotus flower is a magical flower for it is rooted in mud, surrounded by water and somehow finds a way to bloom and grow. A lotus is a survivor; it pushes its way through muddy waters and finds the sunlight. The lotus flower meaning varies from culture to culture. In general, however, the lotus commonly serves as a sacred for purity, rebirth, and strength. Because lotuses rise from the mud without stains, they are often viewed as a symbol of purity. Lotus is the National Flower of India. It is a sacred flower and occupies a unique position in the art and mythology of ancient India and has been an auspicious symbol of Indian culture since time immemorial.

The lotus flower has been used in various cultures. In eastern cultures, it is held as a symbol of purity, enlightenment, and rebirth. Lotus flowers are mainly available in six colors, including white, pink, yellow, red, blue, and purple. You planted lotus should be located in a sunny spot in your pond, in relatively still water. Your container should be 6 to 12 inches below the surface of the water. Lotuses don't start blooming as early in the season as water lilies. A lotus needs several weeks of hot weather to start blooming. This flower has about 18 petals. The tips of the inner petals are peaked and one or two of these tips are deformed. The flower is deep-red in color, has distinct striations, and its most distinguishing feature is its receptacle that turns an earth-tone color. There is a height and size difference also. A standard lotus flower is larger than a water lily flower, reaching up to one foot across. A full-sized lotus plant's foliage and flowers can reach up to 60 inches. Many lotus flowers will change color each day until the petals drop so the color of a newly opened lotus flower may be quite different from the color later in the bloom cycle. Their existence stretches back some 145.5 million years. Lotus flowers even survived the Ice Age (1.8 million – 10,000 years ago). The Ice Age was a time of great geological and ecological change. Most plants in the northern hemisphere became extinct during this era.

Medicinal Value of Lotus:

It's rich in antioxidants and micronutrients and may help slow signs of aging and support heart health, blood sugar management, and weight loss. It's also versatile and easy to enjoy in many different recipes, including snacks, main dishes, and desserts. According to Ayurveda, applying the paste of Lotus petals or Lotus seed oil helps moisturize and rejuvenate the skin. Lotus stem is eaten raw when added in salads. Its salad along with pork and prawns is a delicacy in many popular cultures. Lotus stem curry is prepared by boiling or stir-frying the stem.

The pink tipped lotus *(neulumbo nucifera)* has been used as medicine in Asia, where it is native, for well over 1500 years. (A yellow version *(nelumbo lutea),* which is not traditionally used for medicine, is native to Florida.) All parts of the *nelumbo nucifera* varietal are used for food and medicine. Rich in vitamin B. iron, vitamin C, phosphorous, copper, manganese, potassium, sodium and dietary fiber. Nutritionally, lotus seeds are a rich source of protein and are typically made into soups or roasted with spices for a traditional crunchy Indian snack.

Health benefits of eating lotus root includes reduction in cholesterol, improves digestion, helps to lower blood pressure and also helps to boost the immunity system. Lotus root also helps to prevent some forms of cancer, balances your mood, helps to relieve depression, increases the blood pressure and also helps to maintain the proper enzymatic activity in your body. Lotus root does not have any cholesterol and is very low in calories. Lotus root has a unique mixture of vitamins, minerals and nutrients which are very beneficial for our body.

Lotus root has been used for its beneficial effects for thousands of years. In China, the archaeological remains of this vegetable date back 700 years. Lotus is primarily grown in Asian countries like china, Japan, India, Indonesia and Philippines but is also widely cultivated in

various parts of the world.

Lotus seeds are packed with nutritional elements which make them an excellent choice for a healthy diet. It has a high content of protein, carbohydrates, and vitamins including vitamin B, vitamin C, vitamin A, and vitamin E along with essential minerals like potassium and sodium.

The key benefits of Lotus seeds are as follows:

: Prevents Inflammation

: Low Glycemic Index

: Gluten-free supplement for Protein

: Enhance Kidney health

: Anti-aging properties

: Key to weight loss

Less but not last, that Lotus is a God gift flower to us which is empowered our beauty of Nature.

<u>ROSE</u>

From the earliest times, indeed throughout the history of civilization, people from around the world have held the rose close to their hearts. The cultivation of roses likely began in Asia about 5000 years ago and they have been an intimate part of human civilization ever since. Over centuries, these species of roses have been collected, domesticated, selected and bred to produce the myriad of variety Roses we know and grow today. They have been selected for perfume, color and, more recently, their ability to repeat flower, resist disease, suit cut flower arrangements and bouquets, and perform in a range of climates and garden conditions. Rose flower meanings include love, passion, romance, beauty, discretion, elegance, luxury, and sensuality. On a spiritual level, like a lotus flower, a rose in full bloom represents reaching spiritual enlightenment. Furthermore, the thorns on the rose's stem symbolize the travails we go through on the physical plane, which help our souls to learn and evolve. Because roses have been cultivated for so long and they are loved by people around the world, they are fixtures in the mythology and folklore or many cultures.

Roses are best known as ornamental plants grown for their flowers in the garden and sometimes indoors. They have been also used for commercial perfumery and commercial cut flower crops. Rose is called as the 'Queen of Flowers' as well as 'King of Flowers' this indicates that both kingliness (Majesty, Status and Power) and queenliness (Beauty, Grace and Cultural refinement) are its inherent qualities. No flower surpasses it for its beauty, color and fragrance. In the world full of different flowers, Rose is considered as the symbol of love. They have established a strong base in human thoughts and hearts. That's how they mesmerized us with their beauty and appearance.

Red roses are the quintessential symbol of love. They may be a bit of a cliché, but we've never met anyone who would turn down a gift of a red rose when given by someone who makes their heart go pitter-pat.

White roses are for "a heart unacquainted with love," according to Victorian lore. That means the, purity and innocence of youth.

Pink Rose can express everything from gratitude to admiration to encouragement to sympathy. Mix and match to your heart's content.

Say thank you with deep pink roses. These are a heartfelt way to express gratitude. Cream-colored roses are associated with thoughtfulness. Blushing peach roses say "modesty." Purple roses express a sense of mystery and mysticism, perfect for that friend who is always consulting her astrological charts before making a move.

Simply we describe that:

Red Roses-Love

White Roses-Innocence, spirituality and purity

Yellow Roses-joy and warmth

Pink Roses-Gratitude, admiration, elegance and sweetness

Orange Roses-Pride and intense desire towards someone

Blue Roses-Secret or unattainable love

Lavender Roses-Love at first sight

Black Roses-End of a relationship

Medicinal Value of Roses:

The natural oils found in roses help retain moisture in the skin. This results in your skin feeling smooth and soft. The sugars in rose petals especially benefit those with sensitive skin. Acts as sunscreen: A rich source of vitamin C. Rose petals act as an excellent sun block. The anti-bacterial properties found in rose petals make it an excellent remedy for fighting acne and breakouts. Rose petals dipped in water overnight can also help soothe irritated skin and reduce redness.

The medicinal parts of the plants are the flowers, petals, rose hips, root, root bark and essential oil. Vitamins and Minerals which include Vitamin A, B, E and K and potassium and iron form the key medicinal components. The Chinese use the flowers to prepare a drink which acts as an energy stimulant, blood tonic and also works in case of digestive irregularities. The extract of rose plant especially act as an antidepressant, antibacterial, antifungal, antiseptic, anti-inflammatory, digestive stimulant, kidney tonic and menstrual regulator. Mainly from the family Rosaceae.

Health benefits of Rose: **Helps soothe skin irritation. Soothes sore throats. Reduces skin redness. Helps prevent and treats infections. Contains antioxidants. Heals cuts, scars, and burns. Enhances mood. Relieves headaches.**

Health benefits of Rose:

Tea made from rose petals strengthens the digestive process.
Rose tea is a better way to lose weight and stay hydrated.
Regular consumption of rose tea is good for boosting the immune system and preventing different diseases.
Rose tea is good for expelling toxins from the body.
Its use is excellent for skincare and hair care.
Eating dried rose petals helps in eliminating unwanted body fat and weight loss. Rose tea is very easy to make.
Fifteen petals can be boiled in water for 20 minutes and then eaten with a little honey or sugar. This is good for healthy the Heart.
Drinking one or two cups of rose tea daily is good for a healthy life.
The use of this tea is good for preventing urinary tract infections.

 Rose hips are used in bread and pies, jam, jelly, marmalade, syrup, soup, tea, wine, and other beverages. Rose hips can be eaten raw, like berries, if care is taken to avoid the hairs inside the fruit. The hairs are used as itching powder.

Lastly, Roses are really the pride of our garden as well as the glory of our Nature.

#

<u>MARIGOLD</u>

#The recorded history of marigolds begins with the Aztecs in Mexico, where the flowering plant was used in religious ceremonies and as an herbal medicine. Marigolds, both French and African, are indigenous to Mexico and Guatemala. They were discovered in the early 16th century and brought to Europe and Northern Africa in the late 16th century where they were quickly adopted into gardens. The family name, Tagetes, is derived from a mythical Etruscan deity. According to the legend, the lovers would often hike to the top of a mountain to leave flower offerings for the sun-god Tonatiuh, and to swear their love and commitment to one another. The plants are native to the Americas from Argentina to New Mexico and Arizona. The Aztecs raised the flowers and even bred them for bigger and better blooms. Marigold flowers, which are yellow to orange red in color, are a rich source of lutein, a carotenoid pigment. Yellow: Positive feelings, happiness, and joy. Orange-Red: Love, passion, and romance. Orange: Positive energy and strong emotions. Marigolds in many fiery colors. Orange is the most common, but there are also red, bright yellow, cream-yellow, and almost white varieties. Due to its strong smell, antioxidant content and volatile oils, these flowers can be used to naturally fend off mosquitoes, pests & other insects. For this reason, marigolds are planted at home gardens and also used in extract form in candles. Some Marigold flowers are edible and have been part of culinary traditions for centuries. The Aztecs were said to use Marigolds in several ways, including as a food source. Supplementing your diet with Marigold leaves or flowers, a diluted Marigold tea, or a Marigold supplement will therefore do wonders for eye health. With the increasing calls for restrictions on synthetic colors, natural plant pigments are receiving a lot more consideration as possible colorants in foods. Sometimes referred to as poor man's saffron, Marigolds are natural colorants that add beautiful golden color to dishes. Lutein, extracted from African Marigolds is used as a food colorant in many foods, from baked goods to chewing gum and even foods for toddlers.

Lutein is not only used as a food coloring. It is also used commercially and by hobbyists to dye fabrics a deep yellow. The dye is made of dried and ground flowers, which produce rich, vibrant yellows, green-yellows, and oranges. Marigold essential oils are produced from the flowers using a steam distillation process. The essential oil has a strong, warm, pungent aroma with a powerful fruity undertone.

Nematodes, also known as roundworms and are also called soil pests. Planting marigolds is helpful because it provides a natural defense against the ill-effects of such notorious farming pests.

Medicinal Value of Marigold:

Marigold flowers throughout time have been used for a variety of purposes. Medicinally, they are used as an antiseptic and are even reported to cure hiccups. The plant also contains compounds which make it antifungal, antibacterial and anti-inflammatory. This amazing plant has been a part of treating humans for a very long time. The main medicinal applications of marigold are skin conditions of all kinds, including contusions, bruises and varicose veins. Minor skin injuries and inflammation can also be successfully treated. Marigold ointment promotes wound healing, eczema, and sunburns.

Marigolds are highly valuable for medicinal purposes like headaches, swelling, toothache, wounds and many skin problems. The marigold petals can be utilized as a herbal infusion, topical solution & eyewash. You can also brew it into tea. Marigold is helps in the body's detoxification process by removing all toxic materials that have accumulated in the body. This detoxification not only benefits our digestive system, but also lymphatic system by helping induce drainage & ease inflammation of lymph nodes.

Flavanoids that are present in the flowers of Marigold are said to be linked to the treatment of Cancer due to their anti-inflammatory qualities. For the skin, Marigold has been used to treat inflammation, sensitivity, redness and even dryness. Both its essential oil and distilled floral water are considered highly effective to reduce damage caused by UV radiation and prevent signs of ageing. In Ayurveda, Marigold is considered cooling in nature and thus balancing for Pitta as well as Kapha Doshas. Traditionally, a paste of the Marigold leaf would be applied on the body to treat muscle pain but also acne and sun burn on the skin.

Marigold is rich in Carotenes and Carotenoids – the two compounds responsible for the flower's vibrant yellow color and many medicinal properties. These compounds also serve as precursors for the production of Vitamin A. Lycopene found in marigold is reported to reduce the risk of prostate cancer and heart disease.

So, Marigold is really a gold flower in garden & our Nature.

<u>DAHLIA</u>

#For centuries, dahlias have been a beloved garden plant throughout Europe and North America. With over 50,000 different dahlia varieties that bloom from spring to frost. Dahlia has a rich symbolism that stands for wealth and elegance, and also for love and involvement. It's a perfect flower to express your love! For the Aztecs, Dahlia was a religious symbol, besides food the flower was used in different types of ceremonies. Dahlias are tuberous perennials, and most have simple leaves that are segmented and toothed or cut. The compound flowers may be white, yellow, red, or purple in color. Wild species of dahlias have both disk and ray flowers in the flowering heads, but many varieties of ornamentals such as the common garden dahlia.

Red dahlia flowers are a known symbol of both strength and power. Because of that, you can give them to a sick or recovering friend as a get well soon gift. Red dahlias are also ideal gifting flowers for someone who's about to embark on a new professional career or a new milestone in life. Like other white flowers, white dahlias are associated with purity and innocence. Because of their color, white dahlias are frequently part of weddings and other ceremonies. Pink and purple dahlia flowers are associated with kindness, service, feminine beauty, and grace. Purple dahlias also symbolize royalty and dignity, which makes them the perfect gift for someone you appreciate.

Nowadays, Dahlia was widely used even in economical purpose: in landscaping, in floristry as a cut flower, for the pharmaceutical industry, cosmetic, food and as raw material for the extraction of dyes. Both the tuberous roots and the flowers of this ornamental and medicinal plant are used for therapeutic purposes.

The common garden variety dahlia was once an important root crop and medicinal plant among the pre-Columbian Indians of central Mexico, Yucatan and Guatemala. Its roots were valued both for the nutritious insulin stored inside them and for the antibiotic compounds concentrated in the skin of the tubers. In Pre-Spanish Mexico, tubers were used due to high content of fructose and insulin. Tubers skin is rich in antibiotic compounds. The crushed and mashed up petals are used to provide relief from stings or insect bites. Aztecs use the flowers to treat epilepsy. Flower petals are consumed by adding it to salads. In Mexico, tubers are consumed as vegetables. The tuber extract is used as a beverage.

Due to their bright colors and habit of growing on tall, singular stems, Dahlias tend to carry a meaning of positivity, good energy, and happiness. So truly Dahlia, increase the beauty of Nature.

BLUE PEA

Blue Pea is a plant from the family Fabaceae and is commonly found throughout South East Asia. Butterfly pea flower has been prized for centuries because of the unique, color-changing effect they can create. It is a type of pea, but its flowers are more famous than its fruit. The purple blooms have been used for centuries as a natural food dye. It is still a popular tea enjoyed around the world and an important part of daily religious rituals in India. Butterfly pea flower has been used in both Ayurvedic medicine and Chinese medicine to cure disorders related to memory. It also works wonders as a brain booster and anti-stress agent.

Traditionally, the Butterfly Pea flower is said to be ruled by the planet Venus and connected to the element of water, which gives it the attributes of love, emotion, serenity, and protection. In India, this flower is named after Hindu goddess, Aparajita, meaning one who cannot be conquered or defeated. In Southeast Asia, traditional uses for flowers of the butter fly pea include tea, for dying clothes, and in shampoos for its benefits in promoting hair and scalp health.

Butterfly pea flower tea is commonly used in Ayurvedic and Chinese medicine. In folk medicine, the tea is consumed to aid with pain, inflammation, brain health, eye issues such as conjunctivitis, and to fight some forms of cancer. The butterfly pea flower tea is thought to be a great agent for protecting skin from premature aging from glycation, protein damage from an increase in sugar molecules, and the antioxidants present in the tea can stimulate collagen and elastic synthesis.

Butterfly Pea extract boosts hair growth as it contains a potent bioflavonoid, anthocyanin, which increases blood flow in the scalp, strengthening hair follicles. It is considered one of nature's most effective ingredients for promoting hair growth and darkening hair naturally.

12 Butterfly Pea Flower Health Benefits: Improves Eyesight, Promotes Hair Growth, Improve Skin Texture, Aphrodisiac, Antioxidant, Nootropic, Diuretic, Analgesic, Anxiolytic, Anti-Inflammatory, Anti-Asthmatic, and Anti-anxiety.

Consuming blue butterfly pea tea may have some role in fighting cancers. It enters the cancer cells and inhibits their growth. Anti-inflammatory properties: Consumption of blue butterfly pea

tea can reduce swelling in the body. It can reduce body pain, migraine, and swelling due to wounds and headaches.

<u>JASMINE</u>

#Jasminum sambac is considered as a native of the East Indies. The name Jasmine is of Arabic origin and is believed to have been derived from Yasmin. It is reported that the height of its popularity reached its peck two to five hundred years ago at canton and metropolis of southern China. It is widely believed among botanists that the Jasmine flower originated from Persia, now called Iran. It is said to have been brought across the Red Sea into Egypt in early 1000 B.C. and was later brought to Turkey and Greece. Jasmine originates from the Himalayas and the moderate regions of China. There are around 200 different species, the first of which to be named was Arabian Jasmine, or Jasminum sambac. It is believed that Jasminum sambac, Arabian jasmine, was brought to the Philippines from central Asia in the 1700s. It's little wonder that jasmine has been the national symbol of the Philippines since 1934. Jasmine was chosen to represent purity, simplicity, humility and strength. It also is the national flower of Indonesia, being adopted by Indonesian government in 1990.

To the Chinese, jasmine represents feminine kindness, grace and delicacy, as well as a means of attracting wealth and romance. In Thailand, jasmine symbolizes motherhood, while in India, Jasminum molle, commonly called Indian Jui, is used in Hindu religious ceremonies. Jasmine Flower is one of the oldest and best fragrant flowers. It is considered as the Queen of flowers and is called as the "Queen of Fragrance" or "Belle of India", because of its exclusive scent & excellent fragrance, which soothes and refreshes within a second. Flowers hold a very special place in Indian Culture, as they are intrinsic to so many rituals and customs. Jasmine the queen of flower is associated with love & romance and is also mentioned in the ancient work and Hindu scriptures like the "Mahabharata and Kama sutra".

Many fragrant-flowered plants from other families are given the name jasmine, including the star, or Confederate, jasmine (Trachelospermum jasminoides), Cape jasmine (Gardenia jasminoides), Madagascar jasmine (Marsdenia floribunda), jasmine tobacco (Nicotiana alata), Carolina, or allspice, jasmine (Gelsemium sempervirens), Chilean jasmine (Mandevilla suaveolens), orange jasmine (various species of the genus Murraya), night or day jasmine (various species of Cestrum), and the crepe jasmine (Tabernaemontana divaricata).

This flower can be seen in bridal bouquets as well as garlands on the bride and groom during their wedding day. Jasmine flowers are often paired with another fragrant flower—roses. As white Jasmine also symbolizes purity, it is often used in religious ceremonies from weddings to burials. This flower frequently used in religious ceremonies of the Hindus.

In Thailand, the Jasmine flower is symbolic of a mother's love and conveys respect. In the United States, it is a flower symbolic of beauty and romance. In China, Jasmine flowers signify feminine attributes like beauty, grace, delicate nature, kindness, and sweetness. It is also said to attract wealth, romance, and happiness. The flower is known as the "Queen of the Night" in India owing to the fact that it releases its fragrance after the sun has set. Its fragrance is even more potent during a full moon. It has a relaxing scent that helps in falling asleep. As such it is often planted outside a bedroom window so as to bring the fragrance in from the garden.

The main reason jasmine is so famous is its strong fragrance. People adore the flower for its strong, sweet smell. Countless cultures worldwide include it in aromatic products like candles, perfumes, soaps, and lotions. The antispasmodic qualities of Jasmine make it helpful to relieve indigestion, stomach cramps and soothe inflammation. A recent study found that Jasmine flower extract was effective at inhibiting the growth of Escherichia coli, Staphylococcus aureus and Bacillus cereus. The spiritual symbolization of the jasmine flower is purity, sensuality, modesty, and inspiration. Jasmine is one of the most beautiful flowers found around the globe. It gives a very calm and happy vibe. It is an excellent choice for decoration purposes due to its bright colors.

Medicinal Value of Jasmine:

Jasmine has been used for liver disease (hepatitis), pain due to liver scarring (cirrhosis), and abdominal pain due to severe diarrhea (dysentery). It is also used to prevent stroke, to cause relaxation (as a sedative), to heighten sexual desire, and in cancer treatment. Dried Arabian jasmine is used to flavor tea or for making potpourri. The delicate, fragrant flowers are also used as an antiseptic, anti-spasmodic, sedative and to treat depression. If you have ever purchased jasmine rice, you have realized the powerful effect of aromatherapy. These intensely fragrant flowers have been traditionally used for scenting tea. You can also use these sweet flowers in, obviously, sweet dishes. However, only the species Jasminum sambac of this flower can be eaten as rest all other Jasmine species are poisonous so be careful while picking these flowers.

All parts of the Jasmine plant such as leaves, flowers, and roots are beneficial and are widely used in Ayurveda for treating various ailments. Jasmine helps to lower blood cholesterol levels and maintain healthy heart functions due to the presence of antioxidants. Jasmine leaf extract is believed to strengthen hair's roots, preventing brittleness and enhancing shine. But growing a head of enviable hair is just one small perk of Jasmine. In Ayurveda medicine, it's heralded as a remedy for, well, just about everything that ails you—from a headache and fever to itches and wounds. The important medicinal plant known in America as the 'Carolina Jasmine' (Gelsemium nitidum) is not a true Jasmine, though often called 'Yellow Jasmine. Like most teas, jasmine tea has high levels of inflammatory and antioxidant properties that help to boost the immune system and protect against the common cold and influenza.

Jasmine is used on the skin to reduce the amount of breast milk, for skin diseases, and to speed up wound healing. Jasmine is inhaled to improve mood, reduce stress, and reduce food cravings. In foods, jasmine is used to flavor beverages, frozen dairy desserts, candy, baked goods, gelatins, and puddings. Jasmine is an aphrodisiac, meaning it can heighten sexual desire. That's why it's a common ingredient in massage oils, as well as, of course, perfume, in some countries around the world. The whole flower can be eaten, adding a spicy flavor to stir-fries, chicken or fish dishes. The flowers are intensely fragrant and are traditionally used for scenting tea, but can also be added to shellfish dishes. Only jasmine officinal is edible. Jasmine tea is a natural relaxant for the mind and body. Jasmine is known to have a calming effect on the nervous system, improving restlessness, irritability, and insomnia. The scent of Jasmine can be a more effective sedative than sleeping pills. Jasmine tea is also known to ease muscle tension.

Looking so many properties of Jasmine, it's really a beautiful flower of Nature & its fragrance enhances the beauty of Nature.

HOLY BASIL

For more than 5,000 years, Tulsi (also known as Holy Basil) has been revered as one of the most sacred herbs in India. As Tulsi travelled west along the early trade routes from the Orient to Europe, it became known to the Christians as "sacred" or "holy" basil. Holy basil, (Ocimum tenuiflorum), also called Tulsi or Tulasi, flowering plant of the mint family (Lamiaceae) grown for its aromatic leaves. Holy basil is native to the Indian subcontinent and grows throughout Southeast Asia. The plant is widely used in Ayurvedic and folk medicine, often as an herbal tea for a variety of ailments, and is considered sacred in Hinduism. It is also used as a culinary herb with a pungent flavor that intensifies with cooking. According to some mythological story, it was said that Tulasi is actually an ardent lover of Krishna whom Radha has cursed to be a plant. Hindus believe that every house that has Tulasi plant is a place of pilgrimage and death can never enter. According to the University of New England, the holy basil plant is different from the sweet basil herb because it can help reduce stress and anxiety simply by consuming it. It can help with issues such as depression too as well as aid in alleviating any allergy symptoms you may be experiencing.

Indian holy basil or Tulasi is not used in cooking but in traditional medicine, essential oils and in teas. Thai basil, sweet or great basil is used in cooking. Though both are basil plants, they are quite different in usage.

The main chemical constituents of Tulsi are: Oleanolic acid, Ursolic acid, Rosmarinic acid, Eugenol, Carvacrol, Linalool, and β-caryophyllene, have been used extensively for many years in food products, perfumery, and dental and oral products and plant extract continues the numerous searches for more effective drugs. It grows naturally in moist soil all over the globe. This plant is also grown as a pot herb and in home gardens. Tulsi is cultivated in semi urban areas and the fresh herbage is sold to the temples and worship centers. The major source of Tulsi is from wild habitat including uncultivated field and roadside. The sacred basil is renowned for its religious and spiritual sanctity, as well as for its important role in the traditional Ayurvedic and Unani system of holistic health and herbal medicine of the East. Marked by its strong aroma and astringent taste, it is regarded in Ayurveda as a kind of 'elixir of life' and believed to promote longevity. Tulsi extracts are used in Ayurvedic remedies for common colds, headaches, stomach disorders, inflammation, heart disease, various forms of poisoning and malaria. Ocimum sanctum L. (Tulsi) is an erect, much branched sub-shrub 30-60 cm tall, with simple opposite green or purple leaves that are strongly scented and hairy stems. Leaves have petiole and are ovate, up to 5 cm long, usually somewhat toothed. Flowers are purplish in elongate racemes in close whorls. Tulsi is native throughout the world tropics and widespread as a cultivated plant and an escaped weed. It is cultivated for religious and medicinal purposes and for its essential oil.

Holy basil contains vitamin C and A, and minerals like calcium, zinc and iron, as well as chlorophyll and many other phytonutrients. Also enhances the efficient digestion, absorption and use of nutrients from food and other herbs. Protein: 30 Kcal, 4.2 g; Fat: 0.5 g; Carbohydrate 2.3 g; Calcium: 25 mg; Phosphorus 287 mg; Iron: 15.1 mg and Edible portion 25 mg vitamin C per 100 g. The nutritional and pharmacological properties of the whole herb in its natural form, as it have been traditionally used.

•Tulsi herb is widely worshiped in India.
• It improves the health of skin and hair.
• It also lowers blood sugar levels and its powder is used for mouth ulcers.
• The juice of leaves or concoction gives relief in common cold, fever, bronchitis, cough, digestive complaints etc.

- Tulsi oil is also used as ear drops in case of pains.
- The cosmetic industry uses basil oil in lotion, shampoo, perfume, and soap.
- It is also used in some skin ointments and promoted as a treatment for acne.
- It is used to treat diabetes, obesity and nervous disorder.
- It is useful in stomach spasms, kidney conditions and promoting blood circulation.
- Its seeds are used in curing urinary problems.

There are three different types of Tulsi or holy basil namely.

1. Rama Tulsi:
Rama Tulsi is also called green leaf Tulsi and this is a different type of Tulsi breed that has light purple flowers and has a clove-like scent to it. It consists of eugenol which is usually found in cloves and has a mellow flavor.

2. Krishna Tulsi:
This type of Tulsi is also called purple leaf Tulsi and has a clove-like aroma. It tastes like pepper in your mouth. This type of Tulsi helps cure infections such as throat infections, respiratory problems, earaches and skin diseases. The oil from Krishna Tulsi is used as ear drops. It is also used to cure malaria, indigestion, insomnia and cholera.

3. Vana Tulsi:
Vana Tulsi is a native to India, Sri Lanka, and Northeastern parts of Africa. This type of Tulsi is usually grown for medicinal purposes and it is imbibed into Indian religious beliefs. This type must be protected from freezing and will grow in conditions that have full sun and dry areas. It has light green leaves that are accompanied by a lemony aroma and flavor. Vana Tulsi leaves increases immunity and this is usually used for preparing tea. When consumed in the form of tea, it provides health benefits such as increased physical and mental endurance and adds more oxygen and nutrients to your bloodstream.

#

#

Medicinal Benefits & use of Holy Basil:

#

1. Healthy Heart
Holy basil contains vitamin C and antioxidants such as eugenol, which protects the heart from the harmful effects of free radicals. Eugenol also proves useful in reducing cholesterol levels in the blood.

2. Anti-aging
Vitamin C and A, phytonutrients, in Holy Basil are great antioxidants and protect the skin from almost all the damages caused by free radicals.
3. Treats Kidney Stones
Tulsi acts a mild diuretic & detoxifying agent which helps in lowering the uric acid levels in the body. Acetic acid present in holy basil helps in the breakdown of the stones.
4. Relieves Headaches
Tulsi is a natural headache reliever which can also relieve migraine pain.
5. Fights Acne
Holy basil helps kill bacteria and infections. The primary active compound of holy basil oil is eugenol which helps fight skin related disorders. Ocimum Sanctum helps treat skin infections both internally and externally.
6. Relives Fever
Tulsi is an age-old ingredient for treating fever. It is one of the prime ingredients in the formulation of various Ayurvedic medicines & home remedies.
7. Eye Health
Tulsi's anti-inflammatory properties help promote eye health by preventing viral, bacterial and fungal infections. It also soothes eye inflammation and reduces stress.
8. Oral Health
Tulsi is a natural mouth freshener and an oral disinfectant. Ocimum Sanctum can also cure mouth ulcers. Holy basil destroys the bacteria that are responsible for dental cavities, plaque, tartar, and bad breath, while also protecting the teeth.
9. Respiratory Disorders
Due to the presence of compounds like camphene, eugenol, and cineole, Tulsi cures viral, bacterial, and fungal infections of the respiratory system. It can cure various respiratory disorders like bronchitis & tuberculosis.
10. Rich Source of Vitamin K
Vitamin K is an essential fat-soluble vitamin that plays an important role in bone health and heart health.
As looking so many properties of Holy Basil such a wonderful shrubs which enlightened the beauty of Nature.

CHAPTER-7

Azadirachta indicia (Neem)

Azadirachta indicia, commonly known as Neem, or Indian lilac, are a tree in the mahogany family Meliaceae. It is one of two species in the genus Azadirachta, and is native to the Indian subcontinent and most of the countries in Africa. Neem can grow in many different types of soil, but it thrives best on well drained deep and sandy soils. It is a typical tropical to subtropical tree and exists at annual mean temperatures of 21–32 °C (70–90 °F). It can tolerate high to very high temperatures and does not tolerate temperature below 5 °C (41 °F). It is also highly drought tolerant, and once established, it can survive 7-8 month dry seasons. Neem trees are cultivated and utilized as a multipurpose tree. Nearly all parts of the Neem tree are useful. In many areas, Neem is considered a weed and based on its antimicrobial resistance and other antifungal properties; they are also used in pharmaceutical and cosmetic industries.

The exact native range of this species is obscure, but it is thought to be native to the Indian Sub-continent (India and Bangladesh) and South-east Asia. Locations within which Azadirachta indicia is naturalized include northern Australia, tropical Asia, Africa, Fiji, Mauritius, Puerto Rico, the Caribbean and many countries in South and Central America.

Azadirachta indicia are a fast-growing tree that can reach a height of 15-20 m, though it occasionally reaches 35-40 m. It is evergreen, but in severe drought it may shed most or nearly all of its leaves. The branches are spread wide. The white and fragrant flowers arise from the junction of the stem, normally in more-or-less drooping flower clusters (panicles) which are up to 25 cm long. These branching inflorescences, bear from 150 to 250 flowers. An individual flower is 5-6 mm long and 8-11 mm wide.

The flower is used for reducing bile, controlling phlegm, and treating intestinal worms. The fruit is used for hemorrhoids, intestinal worms, urinary tract disorders, bloody nose, phlegm, eye disorders, diabetes, wounds, and leprosy. The flowering season of Neem varies from place to place. Generally it flowers from January to May and the ripening time of fruits is from May to August. The fruit pulp is edible.

Medicinal Value of Neem Flower:

All parts of the Neem tree- leaves, flowers, seeds, fruits, roots and bark have been used traditionally for the treatment of inflammation, infections, fever, skin diseases and dental disorders. The medicinal utilities have been described especially for Neem leaf. The bark is used for malaria, stomach and intestinal ulcers, skin diseases, pain, and fever. The flower is used for reducing bile, controlling phlegm, and treating intestinal worms. In the Ayurveda world, Neem is a well-known herb that is the key player in different traditional remedies. This tree is a cure for different problems. Having more than 130 varied biologically active compounds, this herb is anti-bacterial, anti-viral, and immune-stimulant. Primarily, Neem leaves are used to treat neuromuscular pains and Vata disorders. Other benefits include blood purification, toxins removal, ulcers, and insect bites treatment. With anti-bacterial traits, it cures burns, infections, and skin problems fast. It destroys those bacteria that pose infections. It boosts the immune system and contributes to fast healing. Neem flowers are an amazing natural antiseptic that can help in cleansing your system in one of the healthiest ways possible. These flowers are white-yellowish in color and are completely safe for consumption. It is available in dried and powdered form in the offseason, but it is best to consume it fresh. Neem flowers are easily available during the month of April-May-June. It is a wonderful remedy for most of your gut issues like bloating, gas, constipation, indigestion and stomach ache. These flowers help in reducing bile production, control phlegm and even treat intestinal worms. Neem flowers can also benefit diabetic patients by reducing the blood sugar levels and also boost the overall immunity of the body. Consuming Neem flowers can also improve hair quality and cleanse your pimple/acne-ridden skin. Neem flowers own sweet aroma just like jasmine. Neem flowers are used in dried, powdered, and fresh form. Neem flowers are also used in the treatment of belching, nausea, anorexia, and intestinal worms. Ayurveda says that its leaves are magical for the eyes and beneficial for treating headaches and skin diseases. Neem oil is effective in treating many skin diseases and great to be used as a mosquito repellent. You can blend it with coconut oil and its application over the body treats different skin issues and makes the skin tone glowing. Being the best healer in Ayurveda, Neem oil is used for the protection of other plants. Only 2-3 drops of Neem oil may give you wonderful hair, these are anti-aging, and you can say no to blackheads with it. Actually Neem is so valuable for us by Nature. Neem flower is naturally glow the beauty of Nature.

CHAPTER -8

Catharanthus roseus (Sadabahar)

\#

Madagascar periwinkle belongs to the Apocynaceae family. It is called botanically Catharanthus roseus. It is a shrub that grows to a height of 1-2.5 meters. Almost all parts of this plant have medicinal properties. It is an evergreen herb or an herbaceous under shrub, quite hardy, biennial or short lived perennial, up to 3 ft height. The stems are green, silky, and glossy with latex. Leaves are simple, oval, oblong or obviate and opposite in position. The flowers in cymose axillaries clusters, are round and flat with an eye in the center. The star like corolla has 5 petals with varying colors (mainly rose & white). This beautiful and elegant plant requires less care, less water and flowers even in the hottest weather. It can be grown in any type of garden soil and useful for edging, ground cover, mass planting, rockery, border; for clothing steep banks and rocks.

Catharanthus roseus, commonly known as bright eyes, Cape periwinkle, graveyard plant, Madagascar periwinkle, old maid, pink periwinkle, rose periwinkle, is a species of flowering plant in the family Apocynaceae. It is native and endemic to Madagascar, but grown elsewhere as an ornamental and medicinal plant.

Sadabahar has long been used in Ayurveda and Chinese medicines and is said to be a time-tested herbal treatment for managing conditions like diabetes, malaria, sore throats and leukemia. Vinca rosea contains two active compounds, the alkaloids and the tannins. Sadabahar also known as the 'ever-blooming blossom' is a well-known flower that has secured its place both in modern medicine and herbal remedies. Although the plant is native to Madagascar, it is found to be growing throughout the world. The flowers of Sadabahar usually come in two varieties, one dark pinkish-purple and the other milky white.

The host of bioactive constituents present in Sadabahar includes reserpine, ajmalicine, catharanthaine, lochnerin, serpentine, lochnericin, vinorelbine, vincamine, and vindesine. Several researches done in the late 1950's suggest two more alkaloids present in Sadabahar, i.e. vincristine and vinblastine are still used in the treatment of certain blood cancers. Extracts from this flower have also found its way as an alternative treatment for grave health conditions like high blood pressure, stroke, Wilma tumor, lymphomas, Kaposi's sarcoma, neuroblastoma, Hodgkin's disease etc.

Health Benefits of Sadabahar:

Regulates Diabetes, Remedies Respiratory Anomalies, Manages High Blood Pressure/ Hypertension, Improves Cognitive Functioning, Augments Skin Health, Regulates Menstrual Flow, Facilitates Wound Healing, And Wards Off Cancer. Since time immemorial, this incredible flower has been in use for its extensive health benefits. Apart from its ornamental use, it has gained immense popularity in modern medicines and Ayurvedic applications for its use in regulating diabetes, enhancing skin health, treating respiratory disorders, managing hypertension and many more. On consuming it in accordance with doctor's approval, one can benefit from the myriad uses of this vibrant flower.

You can also have Sadabahar plant if you have digestive problems. This plant serves as a great tonic for stomach problems including indigestion, constipation and menstrual irregularities. Women who get heavy periods shall consume periwinkle or Sadabahar plant leaves regularly to regulate their flow. This remedy won't cause any side-effects. Besides, chewing Sadabahar leaves or drinking flower tea during menstruation can treat abdominal pain and cramps. You can powder the root and consume it with lukewarm water every morning. You can also chew one Sadabahar leaf multiple times in the day. Make periwinkle flower tea by boiling some clean periwinkle flower petals in water. Drink it once a day.

Sadabahar or periwinkle plant is underestimated. It is seen as just a flower plant but it can benefit your health in a myriad ways. This flower certified itself as beauty of Nature.

CHAPTER -9

Drumstick Flower

Moringa, (Moringa oleifera), also called horseradish tree or drumstick tree, small deciduous tree (family Moringaceae) native to tropical Asia but also naturalized in Africa and tropical America. Flowers, pods, leaves, and even twigs are cooked and eaten. Moringa oleifera is a plant that is often called the drumstick tree, the miracle tree, the bean oil tree, or the horseradish tree. Moringa has been used for centuries due to its medicinal properties and health benefits. Moringa oleifera, commonly referred to simply as Moringa, is the most widely cultivated variety of the genus Moringa. It is of the family Moringaceae.

If you look around you, the boughs of the drumstick trees are full of fruit. This is a tree to which many of us don't pay much attention. Yet this tree was referred to as "miracle tree" and recognized by the National Institutes of Health as the "Botanical of the Year" in 2007, 2011 and 2012. Apart from this, the super food is a rich source of amino acids, with significant amounts of vitamin A, C, and E, calcium, potassium, and protein, which makes for a perfect everyday nutritional supplement. Since Moringa is packed with vitamin A and E, it becomes a perfect anti-oxidant powerhouse.

The drumstick plant originates from Afghanistan, Pakistan, and India, where it spontaneously grows at the foot of the Himalayas. It's a deciduous tree of the Moringaceae family. The Moringaceae genus consists of 13 species of tropical and subtropical herbs or trees. Originated in South West India, drumstick became a popular vegetable in South Indian states. The crop is widely distributed in India, Sri Lanka, Pakistan, Singapore, Malaysia, Cuba, Jamaica and Egypt. Drumstick is a small or medium sized perennial tree of about 10 m height with fragile and corky stem. Flowering in drumstick varies from place to place and is greatly influenced by rain, temperature, humidity, wind, soil temperature, soil moisture etc.

Every street in Indian villages has a drumstick tree (Moringa Oleifera Tree). People in India swear by the health benefits of drumstick leaves, flowers and seeds. The drumstick tree is native to India and other parts of Asia & Africa. A ride around any countryside in India will show you the abundance of these trees. The beneficial properties of drumstick leaves were discovered thousands of years ago. The latest scientific research has also confirmed the benefits of drumstick leaves as herbal supplements. Drumstick tree uses are varied. Its various parts have incredible nutritional and medicinal benefits. Therefore most of its components are used. The parts that are used are: Immature seed pods, called "drumsticks", Leaves, Mature seeds, Oil pressed from seeds, Flower.

Medicinal Benefits of drumstick flower

The nutrition present in drumstick flower are ,Vitamin A (Alpha and Beta carotene),Vitamin B, Vitamin B1,Vitamin B2,Vitamin B3,Vitamin B4,Vitamin B5,Vitamin B6,Vitamin C, Vitamin D, Vitamin E,Vitamin K, Folate (Folic Acid),Iron,Calcium,Phosphorous and Biotin.

Drumstick flowers contain a lot of health and medicinal benefits. Drumstick flowers act as an energizer and are said to treat sexual debility. Drumstick flowers are a great treatment for pox. A table spoon of fresh drumstick flower and leaf with honey and a pint of coconut water is herbal medicine to treat diarrhea, colitis or jaundice, along with other digestive disorders. Drumstick flowers contain antibacterial properties. When boiled in water and consumed as a soup, plays an important part in treating infections of throat, lungs and skin. These flowers are rich in Vitamin B1,B2,B3, A and C which helps in fulfilling the daily vitamin requirement of the body. The drumstick flowers are a very good source for vegetarians and it is said to have the highest protein amount of any other plant situated on earth. Plays a vital role in lowering blood pressure. Consuming drumstick flowers can help in increasing overall body resistance. Drumstick flowers are sometimes used to treat HIV. Contains calcium and phosphorous which strengthens bones. Drumstick flowers contain neomycin which prevents the development of cancer cells.

The leaves of the Moringa tree are the world's most nutrient-rich source of plant protein, containing 92 distinct nutrients and all nine essential amino acids — including methionine and cysteine — compounds rarely found in plants. Moringa leaves can be consumed fresh, dried, or powdered. Moringa helps control blood glucose levels, which can prevent and treat diabetes. Moreover, the leaves are high in protein, which can further reduce your likelihood of diabetes. Moringa reduced their risk of type 2 diabetes by as much as 18%.

Moringa leaves contain many anticancer compounds, including eugenol, niazimicin, and isopropyl isothiocyanate. These compounds are bioactive, meaning they provide health benefits beyond their basic nutritional value. They can kill cancer cells and potentially prevent cancer from developing. Moringa's high iron levels benefit people with anemia. Moringa oleifera is high in antioxidants like vitamin B2, as well as a number of proteins. When used as oil on skin and hair, Moringa can fight damaging pollutants and unstable molecules called free-radicals. Moringa leaves have lots of fiber, which regulates your digestive system. Even as a powder, Moringa is high in soluble and insoluble fibers, the two main types of fiber that not only help digest food but prevent diseases.

#

Drumstick, also known as Shehjan in India has a lot of health benefits to offer. The mysterious benefit is that the flowers of drumstick help to cure the sexual debility in men. Health experts even claim that eating those flowers for 2-3 weeks regularly can help cure impotency, the thinness of semen and premature ejaculation. One of the compounds found these flowers increases the sperm count and helps strengthen their motility. Being one of the aphrodisiac foods, Drumsticks also promote sexual desires without any side effects.

Extracted from seeds of the most nutrient-dense tree on the planet, Moringa Oil is a rich source of powerful antioxidants, vitamins, and minerals that meets all your skin needs. Moringa oil also has a strong resistance to going rancid, and it can stay fresh for many years. It is a special ingredient in revitalizing shampoos, age-defying creams, and many other beauty and health products.

Moringa oil's healing and beautifying benefits were documented thousands of years ago. The Romans and Greeks used this edible oil extracted from the seeds for skin lotions, ointments, and perfumes. In Egypt, Moringa oil was used for protecting the skin against the ravages of sun, sand, and dust during the long travels in the desert. Perhaps this is the reason why people in these countries are admired for their radiant and youthful-looking skin. Moringa Oil helps in cleansing, nourishing, and nurturing your skin naturally. It is often compared to other oils like Olive oil and Argon oil. It provides a protective barrier for your skin, Repairs skin from damage caused by pollution, It works as an anti-aging oil, It brings out the natural glow of your skin, It fights acne, helps in getting rid of dark spots, It cleanses and rejuvenates your skin, It nourishes dry skin, It provides relief from pain and helps in relaxation.

Drumstick and its leaves is undoubtedly a super food, thanks to the immense health benefits we can get from it. In fact, Moringa has been used in Ayurvedic medicine for thousands of years. Naturally Moringa is beauty of Nature.

CHAPTER - 10

Hibiscus

Hibiscus is a beautiful flower. It lasts only for a single day. Hibiscus flower is red, white, pink or yellow in color. The flowers are trumpet-shaped, with five or more petals. Hibiscus is known as the 'shoe flower' because the flowers were traditionally used to polish shoes. The leaves are alternate, ovate to lanceolate, often with a toothed or lobed margin (dentate). The flowers are large, conspicuous, trumpet-shaped, with five or more petals, color from white to pink, red, blue, orange, peach, yellow or purple, and from 4–18 cm broad. Member species are renowned for their large, showy flowers and those species are commonly known simply as "hibiscus", or less widely known as rose mallow. Other names include hardy hibiscus, rose of Sharon, and tropical hibiscus. The most common tropical hibiscus found in nurseries is Hibiscus rosa-sinensis. Different cultivars will give you a choice of flower color and size. They can be very large and showy, with bright and rich colors. Gumamela is also known as Hibiscus. In the Philippines, gumamela is cultivated as an ornamental plant. The gumamela flower comes in many colors: red, yellow, orange, white, purple, pink and other color combinations. Hibiscus, also known as rose mallow, is a plant that belongs to the mallow family

The name 'Hibiscus' comes from hibiskos, the old Greek name for the common marsh mallow. The most commonly grown species is Hibiscus rosa-sinensis, which means China rose. Hibiscus is large, flat, conspicuous, trumpet-shaped flowers. Hiscus flowers have five petals, ranging from white to pink, red, purple or yellow. The species name means rose of China, but experts believe that hibiscus more likely originates from India. An early hibiscus researcher, Ross Gast, sailed the world looking for the plant's true origin. He believed that people from India spread hibiscus south and into the Pacific Islands. Hibiscus contains anthocyanins, which are pigments that give the flowers their vibrant red color. It also has flavonoids, phenolic acids, and organic acids. Many of these compounds act as antioxidants. Carl Linnaeus, who gave us the Latin based taxonomy of plants that became the standard, collected at least one specimen of Hibiscus rosa-sinensis and gave it that name in 1753 when he released his famous books, "Species Plant arum" (Species of Plants). He described a red double flower in that first naming of hibiscus. Hibiscus is generally considered quite a feminine flower and is usually given to or worn by women. In Victorian times, the gift of a hibiscus bloom meant that the giver was acknowledging the receiver's delicate beauty.

White is a common hibiscus color, and, as with many white flowers, a white hibiscus is most commonly seen to symbolize beauty, purity, and femininity. Yellow hibiscus flowers are most commonly associated with good luck and good fortune, but can also symbolize sunshine and happiness. Pink hibiscus flowers are commonly given to little girls. They can be used to symbolize friendship and many kinds of love. Red hibiscus flowers symbolize passion and deep romantic love. Purple hibiscus flowers are usually associated with royalty or the upper class, as many purple flowers are. They can also be used to symbolize knowledge and mystery.

In many parts of the world, blooms from the hibiscus commonly known as roselle (Hibiscus Sabdariffa) are used to make a hot or cold tea. In West Africa, the red, tart drink is known as bissap. It's called aqua de jamaica in Mexico and Central America, sorrel in the Caribbean, orhul in India, karkade in Egypt, and gul e khatmi in Iran. Hibiscus flower meaning often is associated with personal power, fame, and glory. The blossoms may also be associated with wealth. In China Both men and women can give and receive hibiscus flowers. A gift of a hibiscus may indicate that they wish them glory and success. In Hinduism, the red hibiscus blossom belongs to the Goddess Kali and Lord Ganesh. Egyptians believed that the flower was an aphrodisiac and used it to arouse licentious moods. As a result, unmarried women weren't allowed to drink hibiscus tea. As for symbolism, the flowers are often used to represent hospitality. Sometimes, they also symbolize power and respect.It has some amazing properties that can help you in treating your skin and hair problems. Hibiscus is a rich source of hydroxy acids that can make your skin healthy and beautiful. Hibiscus is packed with flavonoids, phenolic compounds, anthocyanins, fatty acids and other pigments that work wonders for hair care - from strengthening the roots to reducing fullness and split ends. It is particularly known for its hair growth-enhancing abilities, and is commonly used as hair oils, shampoos, conditioners, and even hair masks. Hibiscus benefits for hair is , Stimulates Hair Growth, Makes Hair Smooth and Silky, Prevents Baldness, Delays Premature Grey Hair, Hibiscus with natural anti-aging properties help improve skin elasticity and prevent early signs of aging naturally.

Medicinal Value of Hibiscus:

Hibiscus is used for treating loss of appetite, colds, heart and nerve diseases, upper respiratory tract pain and swelling (inflammation), fluid retention, stomach irritation, and disorders of circulation; for dissolving phlegm; as a gentle laxative; and as a diuretic to increase urine output. Nutrition present in hibiscus is Calcium, Phosphorous, Iron, Niacin, Vitamin C, and Riboflavin. Hibiscus contains antioxidants and essential compounds like anthocyanins and flavonoids which come with many health benefits that balance blood pressure, Lowers blood pressure, Lowers blood sugar, and Lowers cholesterol, Improves hair growth, Immunity booster, Prevents skin cancer. Both green tea- and hibiscus-treated group had shown significant nephroprotective effects. They reduced biochemical indicators or nonenzymatic markers of the kidney dysfunction compared with gentamicin-induced nephrotoxicity. Hibiscus tea may be an effective herbal remedy for weight loss. It has shown potential in preventing weight gain, promoting belly fat burning, and reducing fat absorption. Hibiscus, a flowering plant, has been shown to increase uric acid levels in the urine (a byproduct of removing uric acid from the body). One animal study found hibiscus could be effective in lowering uric acid levels, which could theoretically reduce the risk of gout. In a comparison of the antioxidant content of 280 common beverages, hibiscus tea, derived from the flower of the same name and also known as roselle, sorrel, jamaica, or sour tea, ranked number-one, even beating out the oft-lauded green tea. Rosella (Hibiscus Sabdariffa) is considered able to increase the hemoglobin levels in pregnant mothers. Hibiscus tea contains large levels of vitamin C, which can help you fend off the common cold and flu. The effect of sour tea can help boost immunity and keep you healthy, even during flu season. Research studies have consistently shown that vitamin C plays an important role in human health.

Roselle is used in many folk medicines. It is valued for its mild laxative effect, ability to increase urination, relief during hot weather and treatment of cracks in the feet, bilious, sores and wounds. Traditionally in Sudan, Roselle has been used for relief of sour throat and healing wounds. In African folk medicine, Roselle leaves are used for their, antimicrobial, emollient, antipyretic, diuretic, anti-helmentic, sedative properties and as a soothing cough remedy, whereas in India, leaves are poultice on abscesses.

Roselle is medicinal plant with a worldwide fame. Roselle, having various medically important compounds called phytochemicals, is well known for its nutritional and medicinal properties. Seeds, leaves, fruits and roots of the plant are used as food and herbal medicine. Extracts from Roselle plays a crucial role in treating different medical problems including many cardiovascular disorders and Now days so many research going on hibiscus. Looking above this feature of Hibiscus and properties, Roselle gives a pure beauty in our Nature.

CHAPTER - 11

Passion Flower

The name 'passion flower' refers to the passion of Jesus and the genus therefore has a particular relevance at Easter. Spanish Christian missionaries adopted the unique structure of the plant as symbols of the last days of Jesus and especially his crucifixion. The passion flower was discovered by the Spanish doctor, Monardes in Peru in 1569. Forty years later, it was introduced to Europe as an ornamental plant, for, long before the passion flower was included in the Europe's treasury of medicinal plants, botanists were fascinated by this climber's inflorescence. Passion flower is a woody vine that has unusual blossoms. Roman Catholic priests of the late 1500's named it for the Passion (suffering and death) of Jesus Christ. They believed that several parts of the plant, including the petals, rays, and sepals, symbolized features of the Passion. The various elements of the passion flower came to symbolize aspects of Jesus' passion – the final hours before his death. The passion is described in the Bible, in the Gospels of Matthew, Mark, Luke, and John. Passion flowers (Passiflora spp.) are perennial woody vines, mostly from tropical America but with a few species originating in Asia, Australasia and the Polynesian Islands. They climb through the supporting vegetation by means of coiled tendrils. A native of the West Indies and South America, Passion Flower can be smoked as a cigarette substitute, providing a temporary high, or used as a sedative when consumed as a tea.

Habitat destruction threatens some passion vines in their native habitats. The IUCN has categorized 20 South American species as Vulnerable or Endangered. On the other hand, some species have spread outside their native range and become invasive species in other countries. Passionflower is ecologically intriguing, drop-dead gorgeous, and an incredibly useful herbal medicine and wild edible. Passion flower is in bloom from mid- to late summer and, after a warm summer, it is not unusual to find large orange-yellow fruits forming. These can be left on the plants for decoration. They are edible but do not have an outstanding flavor.

Today, passionflower is promoted as a dietary supplement for anxiety and sleep problems, as well as for pain, heart rhythm problems, menopausal symptoms, and attention-deficit hyperactivity disorder. It is applied to the skin for burns and to treat hemorrhoids. Passion flower is native to the southeastern United States and Central and South America. It's been traditionally used to help with sleep. People use passion flower for anxiety, including anxiety before surgery. Some people also take passion flower for insomnia, stress, pain, and many other conditions. How can you take passionflower? You can add dried passionflower to boiling water to create an herbal tea. You can find dried passionflower or prepackaged tea at many health food stores. You can also find liquid extracts, capsules, and tablets.

According to the NCCIH, passionflower is generally considered safe. But it may cause some side effects, such as: sleepiness. The above-ground parts (flowers, leaves, and stems) of the passionflower are used for medicinal purposes. Scientists believe passionflower works by increasing levels of a chemical called gamma amino butyric acid (GABA) in the brain. GABA lowers the activity of some brain cells, making you feel more relaxed. Since GABA affects your mood, many individuals suffering from anxiety try passionflower. You can take a larger amount of passionflower for anxiety. Adults can take up to 90 mg each day to help lessen anxiety.

Medicinal Value of Passion Flower:

Today, passionflower is promoted as a dietary supplement for anxiety and sleep problems, as well as for pain, heart rhythm problems, menopausal symptoms, and attention-deficit hyperactivity disorder. It is applied to the skin for burns and to treat hemorrhoids. Passion flower is native to the southeastern United States and Central and South America. It's been traditionally used to help with sleep. People use passion flower for anxiety, including anxiety before surgery. Some people also take passion flower for insomnia, stress, ADHD, pain, and many other conditions. Passionflower is an extract of the flowers of the plant Passiflora incarnate that is claimed to have natural sedative properties and to be useful for treatment of anxiety and insomnia. Passionflower is a flowering type of vine that's been said to help with insomnia, anxiety, hot flashes, pain, and more. And with over 500 known species of the plant, there's a lot of benefits to go around. Studies suggest that passionflower works by increasing gamma-amino butyric acid (GABA) in the brain. The portion of the vine above the ground is used to make medicine, teas, and other forms of home remedies.

Passion flower tea is made by adding a teaspoon of dried passion flowers to a cup of boiling water or if you're using a teapot, add 2 teaspoons to the pot. What is this? Allow the tea to steep for a few minutes and then strain and sip slowly. If you prefer a weaker tea, reduce the steeping time. Many individuals suffering from anxiety try passionflower. You can take a larger amount of passionflower for anxiety. Adults can take up to 90 mg each day to help lessen anxiety. A native of the West Indies and South America, Passion Flower can be smoked as a cigarette substitute, providing a temporary high, or used as a sedative when consumed as a tea. Up to 800 mg daily of a dried alcoholic extract of passionflower has been used with apparent safety in studies lasting up to 8 weeks, but it may cause drowsiness, confusion, and uncoordinated movement in some people.

Passion fruit is a great source of vitamins A and C, iron, magnesium, and potassium. It's have Calories: 229,Fat: 1.7g,Sodium: 66.1mg,Carbohydrates: 55.2g,Fiber: 24.5g,Sugars: 26.4g,Protein: 5.2g,Vitamin C: 70.8mg,Vitamin A: 151mcg,Iron: 3.8mg,Magnesium: 68.4mg,Potassium: 821mg. The passion fruit is a colorful egg-shaped fruit with numerous small, black seeds that are surrounded by deep orange-colored sacs. These sacs contain the juice that's the edible part of the fruit. The characteristic flavor and aroma makes it a refreshing tropical fruit. There are more than 500 species in this family and more than 50 of them are edible. But only two varieties — purple passion fruit (Passiflora edulis) and yellow passion fruit (Passiflora flavicarpa) — are grown commercially. Passion fruit is a rich source of soluble and insoluble fiber. So it improve our Digestive and Intestinal Health. Extract of passion fruit decreased the symptoms of asthma, including reduction in the prevalence of sputum, cough and breathlessness. The juice extract of the yellow variety exhibits anti-cancer properties owing to its anti-oxidant properties. Passion fruit contains anthocyanins, a group of pigments which gives color to the fruit and reduces the formation of tumors.

Passion fruit's fiber and nutrient content can help promote health. It helps Lowers Blood Pressure, Supports Weight Loss, Reduces Cancer Risk, Promotes Skin Repair, Prevents Iron-Deficiency Anemia, Allergies. From nature, Passionflower is a gift to us. So it's make a place in our beauty of Nature.

CHAPTER - 12

Lavender

#Technically an herb, lavender plants produce gorgeous spike-like violet flowers with multiple tiny purple blossoms. This plant has a soothing fragrance along with a medley of medicinal and culinary applications such as the use as lavender essential oils. The origin of Lavender is believed to be from the Mediterranean, Middle East and India. Its history goes back some 2500 years. Lavender is a flowering plant of the mint family known for its beauty, its sweet floral fragrance and its multiple uses. Lavender is indigenous to the mountainous areas of the countries bordering the western European part of the Mediterranean region. When early travelers brought it back, the plant spread fairly rapidly to other parts of the world, and by the sixteenth-century lavender was already a much-loved plant in English gardens. The name Lavender comes from the Latin word 'lavare' meaning 'to wash'. Many ancient societies used this herb in baths, beds, clothes, on their bodies and in their hair. Over 2500 years ago, lavender was used in ancient Egypt during the mummification process. Back in the Elizabethan times, when baths weren't common practice, lavender was used to perfume clothes and bed linen. The scent of lavender deters mice, flies, mosquitoes and other pests from the area.

The flowers of lavender are fragrant in nature and have been used for making potpourri and cosmetics for centuries. Traditionally, lavender essential oil has also been used in making perfumes. The oil is very useful in aromatherapy and many aromatic preparations. It is known for its antiseptic and antibiotic properties that can kill bacteria, alleviate the effects of bee stings and migraines, heal burns and ward off moths in clothing closets. The fragrance of lavender is also used for calming horses, promoting deeper and longer sleep and balancing emotions. Lavender is frequently used in tattoos to symbolize its healing properties. It can also be used to symbolize purity, love, or devotion to a person or to a cause. Restful, serene and floral, lavender is one of the most beloved scents we use today. Its soft purple buds clustered around a tall sprig symbolize grace, calmness and even luxury. Lavender is so synonymous with serenity that it is associated with the crown chakra, known for its spiritual connection. Lavender has been shown to affect the parasympathetic nervous system. The parasympathetic nervous system controls bodily processes associated with anxiety, such as heart rate, breathing rhythm, and hormone secretion. Lavender can help in regulating these bodily processes by restoring a neutral state.

The main difference between lavender and lilac (colors) is that the lavender is a pale purple with a bluish tinge while the lilac is as a pale purple with a pinkish tinge. Lavender and lilac are two shades of purple and violet. They are very similar to each other and many people often confuse these two shades. Hyacinth. If you love the smell of lavender but prefer something a little less herbal and a little more floral, look no further than the hyacinth – similar to lavender but slightly sweeter, and widely available as a cut flower.

Lavender can be grown in garden beds or in pots. To grow lavender successfully it needs well-drained soil and full sun. In arid climates lavender grows well as a perennial, but in humid climates it is often grown as an annual. French lavender (Lavandula dentata) varieties grow well indoors. They're not as fragrantly potent as English lavender (Lavandula angustifolia), but they adapt better to interior conditions. Lavender needs full sun and good drainage. It is more likely to die from excess moisture than from cold in winter. A pot is an excellent way to provide drainage, though the plant will be more vulnerable to cold temperatures than it would be in the ground. About the only insects you see around lavender are bees. They love the flowers, but other bugs stay away. Lavender has a delicate, sweet smell that is floral, herbal, and evergreen woodsy at the same time. It has soft, powdery, or Smokey notes as well. Some lavenders have a more medicinal camphor smell that is closer to the balsamic resin scent of rosemary.

Lavender flowers represent purity, silence, devotion, serenity, grace, and calmness. Purple is the color of royalty and speaks of elegance, refinement, and luxury, too. The color is also associated with the crown chakra, which is the energy center associated with higher purpose and spiritual connectivity. In all of the mentions in the bible, the lavender is used for purification rituals, for healing, and used as oils and perfumes by high priests and nobilities. It was used in anointing the feet of Jesus by Mary Magdalene. The earlier sources for lavender as it relates to attracting good luck, or possibly repelling misfortune, are linked to its association St. John Day where it was burned in bonfires when evil spirits were said to walk among men. The stunning flowering herb produces beautiful blossoms in hues of pink, white blue and purple and tends to have a peaceful effect on its surrounding. Lavender is believed to bring peace and harmony to the interactions between loved ones and is regarded as a symbol of love, happiness, devotion and protection.

People commonly use lavender for anxiety, stress, insomnia, depression, dementia, pain, and many other conditions, but there is no good scientific evidence to support many of these uses. It is frequently used as an aid to sleep and relaxation. Dried Lavender flowers are used extensively as fragrant herbal filler inside sachets - to freshen linens, closets and drawers. As an air spray, it is used to freshen in practically any room. Aroma therapists use lavender in inhalation therapy to treat headaches, nervous disorders, and exhaustion. Herbalists treat skin ailments, such as fungal infections (like candidacies), wounds, eczema, and acne, with lavender oil. It is also used in a healing bath for joint and muscle pain. Though most lavender is technically safe to eat, culinary lavender is typically cultivated from Lavandula angustifolia plants and has a lot less oil than the aromatic lavender used in perfumes or soaps.

Drinking lavender tea is a great way to induce relaxation and unwind after a tough day. It's packed with healthy compounds that can boost your immune system and alleviate pain by reducing inflammation. Drink lavender tea from flowers in your own garden or opt for pre-dried batches from your favorite tea seller. Lavender is commonly consumed in foods. It's possibly safe when taken as medicine. Side effects might include constipation, diarrhea, and headache. When applied to the skin: Lavender is possibly safe. Some studies suggest that consuming lavender as a tea can help digestive issues such as vomiting, nausea, intestinal gas, upset stomach, and abdominal swelling. In addition to helping with digestive problems, lavender is used to help relieve pain from headaches, sprains, toothaches, and sores.

Medicinal value of Lavender:

Lavender (Lavandula angustifolia) is an evergreen plant native to the Mediterranean. Its flower and oil have a popular scent and are also used as medicine. Lavender contains an oil that seems to have calming effects and might relax certain muscles. It also seems to have antibacterial and antifungal effects. Aroma therapists use lavender in inhalation therapy to treat headaches, nervous disorders, and exhaustion. Herbalists treat skin ailments, such as fungal infections, wounds, eczema, and acne, with lavender oil. It is also used in a healing bath for joint and muscle pain. Lavender contains over 100 known compounds, including phytochemicals and antioxidants. The most well-known of these compounds is limonene, which stimulates digestive enzymes in the liver and may help to detoxify the body of carcinogens. Lavender is also reputed for its calming effects. Both the flowers and leaves can be eaten and have a pleasant yet slightly bitter flavor. Lavender grows throughout southern Europe, Australia and the United States. Dried lavender has only a few calories per tablespoon and is free of fat and cholesterol.

Lavender oil is believed to have antiseptic and anti-inflammatory properties, which can help to heal minor burns and bug bites. Some studies suggest that consuming lavender as a tea can help digestive issues such as vomiting, nausea, intestinal gas, upset stomach, and abdominal swelling. In addition to helping with digestive problems, lavender is used to help relieve pain from headaches, sprains, toothaches, and sores. It can also be used to prevent hair loss.

Lavender have so benefits and used for: Managing Anxiety and Stress, Managing Mensuration Pain And Cramps, Reduces Aging, Remedy for Hair Loss, For Nausea, For Toothache, Remedy For Vomiting, For Menopausal Symptoms, For Depression, For Ear Infection, For Mouth Ulcers, For Preventing Mosquito Bites, For Acne. Looking so many benefits of Lavender, it's really a beauty of Nature.

CHAPTER - 13

Sunflower

Sunflowers have a large flower head, almost black central part which is made up of thousands of tiny florets that later become seeds set in a spiral pattern. The petals are typically bright yellow, although some varieties are orange or red. Its stem is rough and hairy while the leaves large and rough with coarse jagged edges. Sunflowers typically grow to between one and a half and three and a half meters, with some giant variants reaching up to eight meters. The common name, "sunflower", typically refers to the popular annual species Helianthus annuus, or the common sunflower, whose round flower heads in combination with the ligules look like the glowing sun. In Greek, Helios means sun and anthos means flower, thus the name Sunflower. In China, sunflower symbolism extends beyond longevity to include good fortune, vitality, intelligence and happiness. Various faiths have adopted sunflowers to express a symbol of worship and faithfulness, as in the flower's faithful dedication to the sun. Throughout the day, plants use the Sun's light to prepare their food. But not all plants follow the Sun. The stems of young sunflowers contain cells that make them turn towards the Sun's light. This property is called heliotropism. At night, in its absence, the sunflowers face east again, anticipating the sun's return. They do this until they get old, when they stop moving. Then, always facing east, the old flowers await visits from insects that will spread their pollen and make new sunflowers. Those flowers too, will follow the sun.

Annual sunflowers bloom during summer and into autumn. Sow new plants every few weeks and you'll enjoy non-stop flowers until the first frost. Perennial sunflowers bloom for a period of 8-12 weeks with some beginning as early as July and others are finishing as late as October. Sunflowers, as their name implies, grow best in full sun. These plants are native to Central America, and thrive in warm, sunny conditions. In shade, sunflowers won't bloom or produce seeds well. Plant them in late spring where they'll receive 6 to 8 hours of sunlight each day. Sunflowers are native primarily to North and South America, and some species are cultivated as ornamentals for their spectacular size and flower heads and for their edible seeds.

The sunflower has many meanings across the world. Different cultures believe it means anything from positivity and strength to admiration and loyalty. In Chinese culture, sunflowers are said to mean good luck and lasting happiness which is why they are often given at graduations and at the start of a new business. These flowers are unique in that they have the ability to provide energy in the form of nourishment and vibrancy—attributes which mirror the sun and the energy provided by its heat and light. Sunflowers are known for being "happy" flowers, making them the perfect gift to bring joy to someone's day. In the event the stigma receives no pollen, a sunflower plant can self pollinate to reproduce. The stigma can twist around to reach its own pollen. Additional fun sunflower fact: seeds produced from self-pollination will grow to be identical to the original sunflower plant. They are "perfect" flowers, meaning that they have both male and female producing parts. To prevent inbreeding, the pollen producing structure (the anther) forms a tube around the style of the pistil. The pollen is shed to the inside of this tube, and as the style grows, it pushes the pollen out the top. Sunflower, teaching the simplest lessons of life to all those, who might pay attention. We're all beautiful, and we're all in this together. Look at life and people from every perspective. You might see something you've never seen before. Sunflowers symbolize adoration, loyalty and longevity.

It symbolizes faith and adoration for all that is, the true faith and loyalty to something that is much bigger and brighter than themselves. In esoteric Christianity, the sunflower is a symbol of God's love. It relates to self-respect, which means being authentic and embracing your own individuality. A common sight at any church or funeral, sunflowers is another popular funeral flower. They symbolize the light that the deceased person has brought to people close to them while they were alive. In Greek mythology, the sunflower is often associated with the myth of Clytie and Helios. Clytie was a water nymph, and deeply in love with the sun god Helios. The flower itself remains a symbol of good luck and a long, happy life. So, by getting a sunflower tattoo you good be having a good luck charm to protect you and make your life long and happy.

The leaves are used as fodder, the flowers yield a yellow dye, and the seeds contain oil and are used for food. The sweet yellow oil obtained by compression of the seeds is considered equal to olive or almond oil for table use. Sunflower oil cake is used for stock and poultry feeding. Sunflower seeds offer a great source of vitamin E which is an antioxidant and helps to keep your skin and eyes in good health as well as your immune system. As well as vitamin E, they contain vitamins A and B, protein, iron, calcium and nitrogen. Sunflower petals can be used as food ingredient in soups, salads or as a garnish for cakes and cookies to add color and flavor to recipes. Moreover, dried sunflower petals are a great ingredient for herbal tea blending. The crushed leaves are used as a poultice on sores, swellings, snakebites and spider bites. The leaves are harvested as the plant comes into flower and are dried for later use. A tea made from the flowers is used in the treatment of malaria and lung ailments. Sunflowers are able to absorb radioactive materials and other pollutants from the soil without much harm to the plant. This means that in areas where radiation has been high, plants such as sunflowers may be planted in order to help clean up the environment.

Cultures all around the world have been enjoying sunflower seeds for generations. However, many people are unacquainted with the health benefits of eating sunflower seeds. These seeds are a powerhouse of vitamins, minerals, and other important nutrients. They are rich in magnesium, potassium, selenium, zinc, and iron. Studies found that, consumption sunflower seeds linked to lower rates of cardiovascular disease, high cholesterol, and high blood pressure. Sunflower seeds are a source of many vitamins and minerals that can support your immune system and increase your ability to fight off viruses. Sunflower seeds are a healthy addition to the diet, providing essential nutrients and beneficial plant compounds. They are a suitable source of fiber and have anti-inflammatory and antioxidant properties. As a good source of minerals, sunflower seeds may support healthy bones and skin.

Medicinal value of Sunflower:

Medicinal uses for the sunflower utilized by the Europeans include use as a remedy for pulmonary affections; a preparation of the seeds has been widely used for cold and coughs, in the Caucasus the seeds have served as a substitute for quinine in the treatment of malaria. These lovely seeds are rich in mineral zinc (100g of sunflower seeds contain 5 mg of zinc). Zinc is essential to improve sperm density and sperm motility. Therefore, sunflower seeds benefits for males include drastic improvement in infertility. Sunflower seeds is a powerhouse of almost all the vitamins and minerals that are essential for females during the time of their pregnancy and post pregnancy. Sunflower Seeds have a content of Folate which is essential for the production of new cells in the body.

Sunflower leaves have therapeutic properties for curing malarial fever. A poultice is prepared from Sunflower leaves and applied directly to the joints. This helps reduce swelling and curb pain. Drinking made tea from Sunflower leaves can also prevent arthritis. Sunflower leaves are a good relief for gastroenteritis. The leaves are boiled in water and the resultant tea drank giving almost an immediate relief. Drinking tea made from sunflower leaves will also help relieve the inflammation of the gastrointestinal tract caused by bacterial toxins. Drinking tea made from Sunflower leaves helps soothe the chest pain and heal pneumonia. Sunflower leaves are used to treat the respiratory tract. Make tea from the leaves and drink while hot. Plasmodium bacteria is a protozoan parasite the affect humans when introduced into the bloodstream, drinking sunflower leaves tea helps kill this bacteria. Sunflower leaves have a health benefit as wound and ulcer dressings. Sunflower leaves have excellent anti-inflammatory properties that help reduce swelling and inflammation. Crushed leaves of the sunflower plant have wonderful therapeutic properties that work against insect bite poisons, bringing instant relief. A tincture of sunflower leaves, flowers, and other herbs is used with balsamic to heal bronchial coughs. Crushed sunflower leaves are used to make a paste that is applied on the forehead in case of a headache, it helps heal the headache and bring relief almost instantly. Sunflower leaves tea is also a stimulant, that raises physiological levels and increases nervous activities in the body. Sunflower leaves contain Vitamin E and selenium which is a strong antioxidant that helps neutralize many free radicals consumed in food or inhaled in the air. Tea from sunflower leaves helps to protect the body against cancer and other diseases. The tea produced from sunflower leaves and petals is an effective remedy for sore throat. Sunflower leaves make excellent livestock fodder that is both nutritional and valuable easy to cultivate resources. When mixed with sunflower seeds it gets a high protein content, which helps keeps livestock healthy and strong. Rabbit feed is 100% vegetable matter, young sunflower leaves have a high concentration of protein that in addition to the nutritional value in the plant, are rich in other minerals and will keep rabbits both healthy and strong, protecting them against diseases and infections.

The lowermost leaves of the sunflower plant have a high concentration of calcium an essential mineral in strengthening and forming bones. Sunflower sprouts are a rich source of vitamin B mostly Folate which produces folic acid. The tender shoots

of the germinated sunflower seed, when blended with water and left to ferment, produces a sprout that can be eaten raw and is rich in calcium and phosphorus. Sunflower plants have many other uses amongst them making body paints. Sunflower leaves are also mixed with the seeds to make a skin protective remedy that cures and heals skin rashes and helps in itches. Sunflower leaves have several uses that make the sunflower plant an important crop whose benefits go beyond seed oil to medicine and manufacturing. Looking these glowing properties and nature of Sunflower, it's really glow the beauty of Nature.

CONCLUSION

Natural beauty is one with attractive features and looking attractive naturally without any makeup. It means your lips are beautiful without any lipstick or lip balm, your eyes are beautiful without any eye makeup, and your face is shiny without any compact. Everybody has natural beauty. The beauty of nature is somehow immortal, infinite, and eternal. The beauty of nature is perfect reflection of the art of God. Natural beauty may be extinct at the moment, but as "the joy of beauty is eternal happiness", so the effect of that beauty on the mind can never be in vain. Their natural beauty will always draw our attention, but it's their life-giving nature that gives flowers their symbolic power and ultimately reminds us why they are so important to our everyday lives.

\#

\#

www.ingramcontent.com/pod-product-compliance
Lightning Source LLC
Chambersburg PA
CBHW042009110726
48006CB00004B/1024